INDIVIDUAL
VOLUNTEERS TO
GROUPS = FUNDING

INDIVIDUAL VOLUNTEERS TO
GROUPS = FUNDING

WILLIAM C. ANDREAS, MBA

INDIVIDUAL VOLUNTEERS TO GROUPS = FUNDING

iUniverse books may be ordered through booksellers or by contacting:

iUniverse
1663 Liberty Drive
Bloomington, IN 47403
www.iuniverse.com
1-800-Authors (1-800-288-4677)

ISBN: 978-1-5320-9937-3 (sc)
ISBN: 978-1-5320-9938-0 (e)

Print information available on the last page.

iUniverse rev. date: 04/20/2020

PREFACE

I graduated from a small Christian university in the Midwest with a B.A. in business administration, became a real estate broker, and helped to found a real estate agency. At age 22, I became the managing broker over 20 agents. That same year, I purchased my first home, and became a licensed appraiser. Sales came easy for me, but I ended up working way too many hours and got sick. I took life and work way too seriously. I decided I wanted to work any type of 9 to 5 office job in attempt to reduce the stress in my life.

In 1988, I became the executive director of a small, dormant hospital foundation. In addition to the foundation, I also managed the hospital's pharmacy, three physician office practices, and facility rentals. I built up the dormant foundation, created the initial board of director's position description, board officer duties, and a board matrix needed for the selection of foundation board members. I implemented office policies, purchased and set up the donor database, developed procedures, and set up the accounting system to tie into the parent hospital's system. I attended several Indiana University School of Philanthropy development courses on Annual Gifts, Major Individual and Corporate Gifts, Special

Events, Planned Giving, and Grants. I contracted Hillary Lyons Associates to help create a comprehensive development department for a one staff office, which mainly established a volunteer, community-based committee for each giving sector. These committees helped to accomplish much more than a one-person office. In development, I found myself often handling communication, marketing, and advertising, in addition to raising money. It was a small hospital, so I was able to handle all these positions. Within three years, I had secured donations to the tune of three times the amount of development expenses, including my wages and benefits. I implemented a $600,000 capital fundraising campaign myself. The committees and I raised $500,000 for a successful hospital remodeling project. In addition to fundraising, I learned about managing a board of directors, board governance, finance & executive committees, cash flow statements, development plans, budgeting, and strategic plans.

I then moved to work at a larger ($20 million in revenues) not-for-profit foundation. This job taught me how to put what I learned into action. I set up the same system, policies and procedures, and giving sections. That organization paid for a year-long major gift training class, where I truly learned how to ask for and receive gifts up to one million dollars. The year I started, I raised $150,000, and 16 years later, when I left, the foundation was raising almost $1 million a year. I managed a $3.1 million capital campaign during my tenure there. I became a Certified Fundraising Executive (CFRE), which mandates a required amount of knowledge and documented experience in funds raised, hours taught in seminars, a good understanding of the annual fund, fundraising letters, grants, infrastructure, internet and social media, leadership and management, major gifts, marketing & communication, stewardship and special events. It provides a study guide of 20 books and there is a final four-hour exam. I also earned my MBA degree in international business.

I am now in my third job in 30 years, as a development director. I can say that I am proficient at starting from scratch at a new organization and building a full scale fundraising/ development operation. I am attracted to researching and identifying any and all needs of a new organization. Then I search for the right donor, asking for the right amount, at the right time and soliciting donations for the right need/ purpose. If successful, development staff members can make a big difference to an organization. Throughout my career, I have been a member of the local chamber of commerce, local and regional volunteer networks, planned giving associations, and a national not-for-profit organization of fundraising executives.

This book is about setting up a volunteer system to increase organized volunteer groups made up of individuals from corporations, faith organizations, schools, and civic groups that will come out in force to help, and also to provide a sponsorship gift. In my experience, I see way too many small not-for-profits that cannot or will not take a risk and pay appropriate wages to hire an experienced development professional who can easily raise three to five times their total budget within two years.

Often, organizations hire an individual with education but no experience and who just needs a chance to build their career. That was me 28 years ago. I thank the hospital for giving me a chance to have a 30 year-long career in a very respectful position. I am writing these short books to help those with little experience are hired by not-for-profits. I am not a technical writer, but write in layman's terms. I want to provide an inexpensive way for newly-hired, inexperienced development staff members to become successful in fundraising and enable their organization to provide a variety of services to their communities. Most books on the subject provide information in a textbook style, but mine includes my insight as to why and how you should raise funds this way. I am sure there are thousands of seasoned development professionals who could have written this book, but I googled "fundraising" or "volunteering" and could not find a book of this kind. I know that there are a lot of newly-hired development staff members who will enjoy learning so much so quickly.

FUTURE BOOKS

also plan to publish other books for the following development projects.

Annual Gifts: Mass mail, peer-to-peer, website giving, online campaigns, *Benevon

Major Gifts: Honor society, tax credit program, one-on-one requests, corporate

Planned Gifts: Legacy society, memorials, wills and trusts

Grants: Local, state, federal, corporate, faith

Faith: Sponsorships, grants, member gifts, volunteer sponsorships

Special Events: Only two per year to match the missions and area

Comprehensive Grants System

One Staff Comprehensive Development

☐ Annual Gifts
☐ Major Gifts
☐ Planned Gifts
☐ Grants

☐ Faith
☐ Special Events

Benevon, or *Raising More Money* is a series of books written by Terry Axelrod, that leads an organization through a four-point fundraising system to build closer relationships, volunteers and donors.

CONTENTS

THE FUNDRAISER'S HANDBOOK:

HOW TO USE GROUPS TO INCREASE VOLUNTEERS AND FUNDING

INTRODUCTION

The idea of writing a book on how to increase volunteers and funding started when I was contacting East Coast non-profits who used volunteers. I was astonished that many were maintained by only volunteer staff, such as the executive director and a strong board of directors. I was searching for new ideas and found that they were very much in the dark about how to afford just the basic staff to operate the organization. I found myself helping one of the volunteer executive directors by writing policies and procedures of the sponsorship and volunteer project I just started. My first attempt provided some of the essential tactics, but I felt inclined to add to the subject. I worked on and off on the manuscript for three months and now have accumulated approximately 78 pages on how to implement the project. I sent this back to one executive director and she felt that it should be shared with so many more so I decided to get it published.

1

GOALS AND OBJECTIVES

The overall goal of this book is to help not-for-profit organizations increase the number of volunteers, save staff time, and receive additional funding.

The process that I am introducing will increase the number of volunteers, and actually shifts staff from communicating with and organizing individual volunteers to organizing them into groups from corporations, churches/temples, schools, and civic groups. The process will work whether your organization uses an online volunteer registration system open to the community or good, old-fashioned paper registration, via walk-in, phone, or e-mail. I am not suggesting that you eliminate registering individual volunteers, but steer more energy to identifying and signing up groups. In time though, to be more successful, you will begin to devote your time to seeking groups of volunteers.

Not-for-profit organizations usually do not have enough staff members to cover their operational needs. It takes just as much time to communicate with one individual as it does to communicate with one volunteer who represents a group of 10 to 100 volunteers. This process will shift your time to conducting one-on-one meetings with representatives that can bring in a whole group of volunteers. Over time, your organization will change from recruiting and working with individual volunteers to recruiting and working with teams of volunteers which will increase your total number of volunteers while saving staff time.

The possibility of getting funding increases when your organization registers groups rather than individuals. Of course, volunteers may donate following mass mailings/solicitations, or in the case of special fundraising events. A corporation may have funds in its advertising budget, community outreach budget, or social responsibility budget, which may be donated to your cause. Churches may have the same, or conduct a "second plate offering" during service, or have grants available for special causes. Civic groups are in business to raise funds to give to their top priorities. Schools and universities usually do not have funding per se, but the students can get very excited by a cause that impacts something with which they are familiar, and they may be happy to pitch in to raise funds for a single large gift or a peer to peer set-up. Sponsorship, along with volunteering, can happen and it adds to excitement of the volunteer day and the devotion of the volunteers who participate.

2

INDIVIDUAL VOLUNTEERS

Organizations that use volunteers in day-to-day operations usually maintain what I call an individual volunteer system. When I was the executive director of the hospital foundation, I also oversaw the volunteer operations. I employed a part-time volunteer coordinator who managed 250 volunteers. She created volunteer position descriptions for every department of the hospital, reviewed applications, conducted criminal checks, hosted orientations, and revised the volunteer handbook. A volunteer department is a cost to any organization; however, think of the cost savings when adding up the potential wages of regular staff. Most of the positions were crucial, and without volunteers, it would have taken at least 70 paid staff members to cover them. For example, 70 positions, 365 days a year for 8 hours a day equals 25,550 hours at an average cost of $10 an hour, for a total cost of $255,500. Maintaining a volunteer program is a very serious business for not-for-profit organizations. The actual cost for the hospital to maintain the volunteer program was $30,000 for wages and benefits for the coordinator, plus volunteer software fees, volunteer smocks, badges, pins, volunteer holiday party, advertising, etc. It cost about $40,000 to save $255,500 and greatly improved hospital services. I don't think that my proposed team or group volunteer system would work for volunteer needs of organizations who use volunteers in day to day operations, like a hospital.

3

TYPES OF SPONSORSHIPS

I introduce a way for a not-for-profit organization to request
sponsorship gifts from corporate, civic, school/university,
and faith sponsorships to help fund a volunteer project. I
want to spend a little time in describing these sponsorship
gifts. A sponsorship gift is different than a gift from an
individual. Individuals give from their hearts toward the
mission of their choice. Individual donations come from
their own earnings net all personal expenses. Of course,
individuals can receive tax benefits, but rarely do individuals
give for the tax benefits only. A true donation is one where
nothing is expected from the gift, but to forward the mission
of the organization. Sponsorships most often are a trade-off.
Let us examine the different types of sponsorship gifts and
the normal trade-offs. I also provide an outline of how a not-
for-profit can design a project which provides those trade-off
amenities in which the donating organization expects.

Corporate Sponsors

Corporate sponsorships usually come through the following levels: International, national, regional, state and local branches. Development professionals can easily research what levels a corporation currently gives via the internet. In addition, giving levels can also be identified through a one-on-one meeting with a corporate representative. Savvy development professionals can request and receive gifts through one to three channels if they plan correctly.

Corporate Sponsors: Marketing Expense

Corporate sponsorships also stem from three main channels. First, donations can be requested from the marketing or advertising department. These types of donations are mainly a corporation's way of doing business, and not so much a gift. Here, a not-for-profit must have ways to promote the donor as a result of the sponsorship. It is an exchange of funds to help each other. This level of giving provides the not-for-profit with a business relationship. Often, if you build a great relationship with a manager of a department like advertising, public relations, or marketing, you can gain a donation. Donations are a result of the development staff members' personable skills to simply meet, talk, make friends quickly, and empower others about the mission and request a donation. Through this type of channel, the entire corporation can give up to a thousand different causes by allowing a or a few staff to choose where their money goes. It is best to identify these types of departmental gift methods. They are based on personal relationships. My favorite sponsorship is where I meet the local branch manager or director of a corporation and build a solid relationship, where I can meet him/her and request a gift and get it the next week.

Corporate Sponsors: Social Responsibility

Second, corporations develop a social responsibility statement as a part of their mission. They carefully plan what social issues they want to help solve through their giving. Top organizational executives recognize the major cost of giving through local levels. In this fashion they may end up giving less, but are more focused on the causes that they want to help. These gifts are from the heart of the company. If a corporation gives through this method, all gift requests are sent directly to one national or international department from all local, state, and/or regional offices. It is a way to funnel donations toward the corporation's chosen causes. Sometimes the corporation expects recognition or promotion for its donation, but not always.

Corporate Sponsors: Grant Request

Finally, some corporations actually form a foundation where corporate earnings are tithed. This type of giving process is more objective, stemming from a grant request rather than building a relationship. Simply follow the guidelines and submit a request.

I have found that by creating a sponsorship opportunity

with your volunteer activities can project an alternative way for corporations to give. Historically, corporations give to special events because of the promotional value and the tickets to the event. In one of my initial meetings with a local corporate leader, he said, "Now this is a project that we would be proud to sponsor. I am tired of 'rubber chicken' dinner dances with silent auctions and golf scrambles. Now, 100% of our donation goes to the mission and our employees will back the project by volunteering." It provided me with a new way to encourage more corporations to give. Today, I have 30 corporations who prefer to sponsor a special event and 30 who would rather sponsor a volunteer club project. A development professional must learn the levels, channels, and benefits of organizational giving before he/she can even begin to solicit funds for a volunteer day project.

Sponsorships: Civic

Civic organizations, like the Elks, Eagles, Rotary, and Lions Club, were founded to support one or more social causes, such as education, veterans, children, health, etc. They are often willing to help others, like your not-for-profit, achieve fundraising goals. Research the organization you are interested in approaching for sponsorship, and learn about its mission first. These groups raise money through food sales, bar, membership drives, special events, and sometimes even gambling. I simply ask to speak at the group's regular meeting and describe my not-for-profit's mission and suggest ways they can help, like volunteering and/or giving a sponsorship gift. Ask the leader for a follow-up meeting. Most likely nothing will happen after your presentation without a follow up meeting with the leader of the group. A one-on-one meeting usually depends on your staff member's personal skills. You may also gain an approach to a civic group by way of being friends with a member.

Sponsorships: Faith

Requests to faith organizations, such as churches, are different from others. In my first year as a Development Director, I met the leaders of 60 faith organizations and got nowhere. After all that work, I gained only two additional volunteer groups and sponsors. I find that in attempting to get faith organizations onboard for any type of volunteer activity, it is best to go from the bottom to the top. You have to find a person who is a member of that church or temple, or mosque and who also supports your organization's mission and services. Now anytime I meet donors, volunteers, or sponsors, I ask which faith organization they belong to in the community. I ask if their organization does community outreach projects, and get the name of their community outreach chairman. I ask if they could arrange a time for me to meet that person. I have a different request package for a faith organization, which is in addendum A. It is patterned after the faith-based relationship of our organization. Many not-for-profits do not associate with faith groups so the following information is irrelevant. See Addendum A for request materials.

ADDENDUM A PAGES: FAITH

(The LMB Beach Association)
Faith Partnerships Registration Form
How your congregation can serve our mission and achieve your outreach goals!

Check the # of the options that you have interest in discussing

Increase the Awareness of (The LMB Beach Association's) Mission.

_____ Invite staff to speak in a service or gathering.

_____ Include materials in Church mailings.

_____ Display materials where they are accessible to the congregation.

_____ Send a Facebook post and/or set a link to (The LMB Beach Association) website.

Help Recruit Applicants or Places to Serve for (The LMB Beach Association) programs.

_____ Invite (The LMB Beach Association) to any church events to host an informational booth.

_____ Provide training for Church office staff to become an educated referral source.

_____ Host a special (The LMB Beach Association) event.

Increase (The LMB Beach Association) (Beachcomber Club) Volunteers.

_____ Sponsor a congregational (Beachcomber Club) one-day project.

_____ Sponsor a congregational multi-day (Beachcomber Club) project.

_____ Create a special women, youth (+17) or other type of (Beachcomber Club) project.

Help (The LMB Beach Association) to fund more beach cleanings, equipment and supplies.

_____ Host a Youth House Bank coin drive.

_____ Set up set annual pledge amount and provide a monthly tithe.

_____ Start a second passing of the offering plate.

_____ Invite (The LMB Beach Association) to submit an annual grant request. (if available)

_____ Host a personal peer to peer online giving site.

INDIVIDUAL VOLUNTEERS TO GROUPS = FUNDING

Name of Faith Community _____

Denomination _____

Contact Name _____

Mailing Address _____

Faith Leader Name and Title
_____Phone:_____

Contacted: □ By Phone   □ In Person   Date _____ E-Mail _____

Referred to_ _____ Title _____Phone: _____

Contacted: □ By Phone   □ In Person   Date _____ E-Mail _____

Interested in Building on Faith Participation this year? □Yes   □ No
     If "No", should we contact next year?   □Yes   □ No

Refer to the Options on Page 1

Awareness Options # (s)___   Mission Projects # (s) ___   Volunteers # (s)___   Funding # (s) _____

Project Date Requested _____ Second Choice _____ Third Choice _____

Describe Awareness Project _____

Describe Service Recruitment Project _____

Describe Volunteers Project _____

Describe Funding Project _____

Project Date Requested _____ 2nd Choice _____ 3rd Choice _____ 4th Choice _____

Contact Name (for staff coordination) _____

Contact Phone #_____ Email: _____

Other Key Church Leaders, Title, Contact information
_____
_____
_____

Sponsorships: Foundation

Foundation sponsorship gifts of event or volunteer projects are far and few between. Again, research the web page of the Foundation. See if there are program, unrestricted, operating, or event sponsorship grants. If so, the materials you present should weigh heavily towards your programs, which serve the community. Promote the volunteering project as a way that helps your organization achieve its mission; maybe have the foundation sponsor a portion of an already established volunteer project.

Sponsorships: Education

Many high schools and universities now require students to complete a certain number of hours of community service. This can be a double edge sword. I find most of the students are very passionate about volunteering and making a difference in the world, but others just want to complete their graduation requirements and nothing else. The trick is to find the head of the school's community outreach program, who can help you organize the different group volunteer days. If not, you can have 43 different university groups registered in an organization. The community outreach director can serve as a liaison between you and the volunteer groups, and coordinate the volunteers. I usually attend one of the group meetings with my laptop and get everyone registered at once. High school and university student volunteers can really increase your volunteer base, and if you work with the right person you will gain return volunteers. The best way to receive a sponsorship gift from and educational unit is to form a team and host a peer-to-peer online giving platform, by utilizing one of the many free online crowd-sourcing software programs. An online giving platform actually provides a great way to raise additional sponsorship funds, empower volunteers, and promote your mission, and it's perfect for schools and universities. Teams can come from all levels of education, from grade school to university, and from different school clubs. It's like when you receive a text or e-mail from a friend who is walking for a cause and asks you for a pledge, such as a dollar for every mile he/she walks. The e-mail may contain photos related to the mission and information about the walk. There is always a call to action with a large "DONATE HERE" button to click, which links potential donors to the organization's website to make a pledge. Invest some time in creating your peer-to-peer platform and offer it as an option for organizations that want to join, but do not have the ability to fund a volunteer project. In addendum B, I provide standard procedures and guidelines for implementing a peer-to-peer online giving campaign.

ADDENDUM B PAGES: PEER-TO-PEER

LMB Beach Association Beachcombers Club Peer-to-Peer Fundraising Tool

This pages is an example of how to present a Peer-to-Peer platform for individuals or groups to fund their project.

We are very excited to announce that now organizations who do not have the funds to provide a sponsorship can still participate in the new Beachcomber Club project.

Organizations will meet with the Director of Development to select a day and send in their logo.

(The LMB Beach Association) will send you your logo (Beachcombers Team Campaign) created on our Peer-to-Peer fundraising site."

One of your employees will register and become captain of the Peer-to-Peer team page, and then the team captain will send the team page request with instructions to the team volunteers. The volunteers will take five minutes to join and select your team, then share on Facebook, e-mail, Twitter, etc. It really works! It will be exciting to see so many friends willing to help you volunteer.

To qualify to be a part of the (Beachcomber Club) project, all members of the team will need to complete this process. All team participants will receive lunch and a free t-shirt just for registering, even though sufficient funds may not have been raised.

Ideally, team campaigns should start their Peer-to-Peer campaign 30 days before the volunteer project and end 30 days after the volunteer project. Incentives will be based on the Peer-to-Peer reports for persons and team totals recorded as gifts.

Personal Incentives:
Register and send out Peer-to-Peer Team Page: Free lunch and t-shirt
Raise $100: Beachcomber flip flops
Raise $250: Beachcomber ball cap
Raise $350: Beachcomber towel
Raise $500: Beachcomber swim trunks or bathing suit
Raise $750: Beachcomber umbrella
Raise $1,000: Beachcomber chair

Lunch and t-shirts are presented the day of the project. Personal incentives will be provided after the project when fundraising results are in.

Team Incentives:
The top Peer-to-Peer group for each period will be awarded prizes TBA.

4

TYPES OF VOLUNTEERS TO SUIT YOUR NEEDS

Now that I have defined where you can gain support of your volunteer activities and the regular individual volunteer system, let me define what types of volunteers you need in order to create a club for the community. Not-for-profits who utilize groups of volunteers will be able to use this process. Organizations (like hospitals) that use volunteers in daily scheduled positions will find it difficult to create a club which a sponsor can support. These organizations are better off requesting gifts from corporations, civic groups and foundations for the entire volunteer program. A not-for-profit must have a specific mission-related activity in order to recruit volunteers. You need to make it as easy as possible for a corporation, faith group, school/university, or civic club to select a specific time period, which can be for an hour, a day, a week, or longer, but a with a specific start and end time. The project/activity should be a regularly-occurring one during the regular workday of this organization (such as eating lunch with a schoolchild once a week, from August through June; or leading activities at a local nursing home twice a week). It really would not be feasible to form a volunteer club and get a sponsorship gift for a once-a-year project. Creating a CLUB is a very powerful mission because everyone wants to belong to, and be a part of something. It's part of human nature. Examples of clubs, programs, and volunteer teams that could create a volunteer club are listed below.

The Restoration Club offers a team of 20 volunteers to clean streets from a rainstorm for 8 hours the day after each storm (this can be further specified by level or type of storm: Level 3 hurricane, for example; or Level 2 twister).

The Revive Club offers a team of 15 to plant, clean, or improve land at a certain place (such as a local park or empty fields in a specific area of town).

The Dog Pen Club offers a team of 15 to wash all the dogs in a pound/humane society in four hours.

The Repair Club offers a team of 20 volunteers to make repairs on homes or other facilities for a day.

The Builders Club offers a team of 10 to help build a home for 8 hours (can be a one-time effort or meet monthly).

The Host a Highway offers a team of 30 to help clean trash off of the sides of a highway in 4 hours.

I think everyone wants to help and volunteer and it is the not-for-profit's business to provide an avenue for him/her to do so. Think of someone waking up and deciding they were going to buy 1,000 tree starts, then driving and finding available land on which to plant them, knowing exactly what type of trees that thrive in that area, buying the tools, having proper fertilizer to aid growth, rounding up food and water for the day, and finally doing the work. Again, it is up to the not-for-profits to plan accordingly to provide housing, tools, training, and staff to monitor safety and quality and the area or clients to be served. You will have to organize all this when you establish your volunteer club: determine how many volunteers will be able to serve at a time, what the group will attempt to achieve, the location, and the time. Your organization will need to be ready for the volunteers to come and serve. Most of you already have your volunteer programming in operation and will not need to do much in this aspect. You will need to be creative in creating a name, logo, and promotional materials to show what you have to offer to potential donors.

5

GETTING STARTED & PROMOTION

always feel a certain amount of risk when implementing a new giving appeal. I try to think about how much more funding you can receive from donors with very little potential loss. Now that you have researched your organization and understand where you need volunteers, you can create your new Volunteer Sponsorship Program. You need to have a good understanding of the potential origin of groups from within from corporate, civic, educational, and faith sponsorships. Promotion is very important to the success of the new giving program. The more you can inform and explain your non-sponsored and sponsored groups to your community, the better. It shows the community that your nonprofit is active and you have many groups interested in contributing to and supporting your mission. I follow my organization's branding strategy, which lists the font style, type, and sizes to use, along with PMS colors, and mission statement, and logo.

First, establish a name for the club. Be sure it suits the organization and type of service, your location, and other elements; for example, if your organization cleans the Pacific Coast beaches, then call it the Beach Bum Club, or Sandy Sandals, or something creative and empowering. Then utilize the volunteer group's name into all promotional materials, such as in all social media, news releases, etc. You may need to utilize a marketing firm to create a logo for the project so that you can simply cut and paste it into all of your materials. You or a staff member may be able to create the logo with the help of Microsoft Publisher or a similar program. I normally work with a local graphic design company to establish a subset of names of development projects, each with its own logo (which is similar to the other giving projects in terms of color schemes). For every new giving appeal that I create in Annual, Major Gift, Grants, Planned Giving, and Special events, I create what I call a one-on-one presentation, usually in a PowerPoint or Publisher software program that incorporates the new name, logo, colors and themes. Sometimes I will create a basic tri-fold marketing piece. Have an advertising agency or graphic design company create logo files for paper, and electronic versions to fit Facebook, web, Constant Contact, Peer to Peer, Twitter, press releases, magazine articles, and other types of media. Create a separate file to hold these original files. Then you need to create the promotional and donor request materials. Provide information about how to register, how to sponsor, and the sponsorship/donation levels, and the amenities received for a sponsorship. I do not have a budget for marketing. I use any and all resources available to inform the community. Your organization will need to risk ordering giveaways for the donors, like trophies, t-shirts, banners, and

6

ORGANIZATIONAL GROWTH & CHANGE
WITH A NEW VOLUNTEER PROGRAM

If your organization's goal is to increase the amount of volunteers and funding, then you must inform department leaders and establish a plan to handle the growth and changes. I find that organizations who utilize a large amount of volunteers to provide their services have a hard time growing because there are certain elements that need to increase at the same time. The elements that need to grow at the same time are funding, staff, clients, volunteers, and the services rendered, materials/tools and promotion. Services rendered can include saving animals, providing services for the disabled, home repairs, cleaning land, planting forests, etc. Development funding and other revenue departments can grow at a faster pace. Money can be saved to fulfill the need in other areas. It is really hard for small and large corporations to introduce a new program, but it can be very rewarding. This program attempts to increase volunteers and funding at the same time. The staff person proposing the change must totally believe in the changes he/she is ready to implement. He/she must have a solid vision and plan to execute them so that all the other players will believe in the change too. The change must come with new policies, procedures, and training for all the players. It is best to go over these and gain full support from the Board, CEO, or president of the organization. In my second month as being the new Development Director, I announced that after 26 years of using volunteers, we were now going to also ask for a sponsorship fee. The staff acted like I was crazy. They said that they actually did not think it was ethical. No one around the table felt that it would work. All it took was that the president spoke up and said that is the new direction that the organization is heading toward and it will be a new way of life for all staff. A year later, I had signed up 52 organizations, 50 percent were new one-day volunteer groups, and 40 percent were sponsored, for a total of $35,000. It works.

Keep in mind that several tasks will need to change at once, and note that there are always new problems with an increase of volunteers that will affect several departments. If there is a major increase to the number volunteers, then the volunteer coordinators have to quicken their processes that prepare for the days of service, like adapting the ordering of materials and volunteer supplies. Since there is now funding by the group, the volunteer coordinator also may feel more pressure to ensure that a sponsored group has both quality and quantity of work. There will also be more pressure on the staff responsible for new applicants, areas to serve, or qualified recipients of service. They will feel pressure to increase the number of applicants or service areas because of the additional volunteers needing projects. The increasing number of volunteers can even affect the communications/media relations/PR department, which issues press releases to local media for each event. There were so many other things that caused heartburn, but after a year all seemed to calm down. Introducing a new giving and volunteer appeal represents major change and growth. It is best to create very specific plans to implement these changes in the organization.

ADDENDUM C PAGES: GROWTH

The elements that need to grow at the same time are funding, staff, clients, volunteers, and the services rendered, materials/tools and promotion.

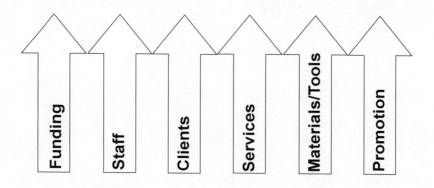

7

POSSIBLE EFFECTS ON REGULAR VOLUNTEERS

Consider how the new volunteer program will affect the regular long standing volunteers. Increasing the number of teams that come out to help your mission can create friction with the regular volunteers. When an organization shifts from individuals volunteering to groups volunteering, a change in the atmosphere of the volunteer program is going to happen as early as the sign-up process. If you create or add new volunteer project days for your new groups and new areas where you normally have not hosted projects, then it won't happen as fast. If not, you are going to be filling up time slots normally filled year after year by long-standing volunteers, who will resent these changes. They will need to be informed that they need to reserve their volunteer days quicker, or put them on a regular schedule. What happens is that it puts pressure on your groups to get their act together quicker. It puts you in better control. Promote the fact that organizations are also sponsoring days. We try not to put a paid group ahead of the regular non sponsored groups or as a special category, but provide them with equal respect. We will save dates while a sponsor group decides, which can take days off the schedule for a period of time.

Some of the long-term, or regular volunteers may want to begin to sponsor their project days too. In fact, you need to circle back and set meetings with them to make a request. Some call in late, as usual, and are shocked to hear that their chosen days are filled. I do not know how well the community supports you with volunteers. If they flood in everyday you need them, then this project may not be what you need. Ours is not the case because we need more volunteers and also funding, and we need to gear up our project schedule. We are now at a point where volunteer groups are signing up in a year in advance.

8

POLICIES & PROCEDURES

This is the most important section of the book. Here, I lay out a plan to shift your organization from accepting individuals as volunteers without any funding to forming organized groups with a sponsorship gift. I actually did not invent this project from scratch. I listened in on a monthly development conference call, which detailed the overall basic program presented by another region's not-for-profit organization. I then created my organization's plan, materials, policies & procedures, etc. I have customized many good development projects from others' projects. I would invite you to subscribe to the e-mail list of a fundraising/development organization and review each conference call and at least take the ones that concern funding projects. To be successful, you must follow the outline given by those who have been successful. Even though there are many not-for-profits who utilize this same process, I have talked to many small not-for-profit organization leaders who had no knowledge about it. Again, this is the sole reason for my book.

Below is an example of policies and procedures that your organization may change based on your needs.

The organization of XYZ adopts the _____Club, which is an effort to increase funding for services and to increase the number of volunteers from current or new organizations. The XYZ organization always welcomes non-sponsored groups to help provide services, but the new rules are in place to carefully manage a balance of your organization's financial and volunteer needs.

Most often, groups are from corporations, churches/temples/mosques, schools, neighborhood associations, and civic organizations. If there is a lack of staff, one volunteer can perform all of these functions of a Development Director, Development Coordinator, and Volunteer Coordinator. The organization that adopts the program can title the paid or volunteer staff members who maintain the new program.

1. Any group that would like to volunteer for a day of service must discuss it first in a one-on-one meeting with the Development Director (DD), to ensure that all the giving options are explained to the group. The DD will then email the Development Coordinator (DC) to notify him/her if the group is a Sponsor or Volunteer Group, and provide group name, contact information, and project date so that the DC can follow through with communication and registration until the project is finished. A team captain should be identified in the meeting.

2. The DD will communicate with the team captain to schedule their volunteer date/time if it has been yet. Then follow up with the team captain to see if enough volunteers are available to establish a group.

3. Once a _____ Club volunteer day is booked, the DC will communicate with the team captain of the group. The DC will send .pdf waivers or create a landing page if they use a volunteer software program, and will instruct the team captain to forward it to the rest of the group. The team captain should work to get all the volunteers registered so the DC can begin to communicate with all the volunteers.

4. All sponsored _____ Club members or non-sponsored groups are required to sign a paper waiver for release of liability, or sign it via an online volunteer software program. Instead of using paper waivers, some organizations require that volunteer use an online volunteer software program and its electronic waivers. Since a waiver is a legal document, it must be completed by the volunteer unless he/she is having technical difficulties, then staff can help them sign up or sign them up for them.

5. The DC normally sends final communication as to where the project/volunteer site is located and, if possible, what type of work volunteers will be doing no later than three days prior to the event.

6. Optional: Single day _____ Club or non-sponsored groups may not work in shifts. All volunteers are expected to begin work at the same time and end at the same time. The volunteer site

supervisor provides work assignments and safety instruction before work begins. He/she cannot stop supervising other volunteers to orient late-comers.

7. Projects longer than one day can have half-day shifts, but must provide a trained person to help check the volunteers in and out during shift changes, using the volunteer software program.

8. We recognize that there are times where volunteers need to leave early. No more than one-fourth of the group can do so, but if fewer than five (or whatever number you decide) volunteers are left on site, work may be suspended at the discretion of the site supervisor.

9. Groups who utilize the a peer to peer fundraising tool to conduct a _____ Club event must register onto their site at least two weeks before the volunteer day. All participants and even other employees and friends may help raise at least $000 two days before the event. All groups will receive a free lunch and t-shirt. Participants of the peer-to-peer fundraising program will receive their amenity gifts even if the group does not raise the total amount. (see addendum B for sample amenities)

10. All volunteer groups that are cancelled due to weather can reschedule at the earliest possible date. Groups that cancel due to low turnout will have to wait until the next calendar year to reschedule.

11. Non-sponsored groups can select no more than three Thursday-Saturday blocks (or whatever days you

choose) to volunteer so that there are opportunities for sponsors to volunteer.

12. Sponsored groups can volunteer multiple times a year at a gift level for _____ Club at $X,000, $X,000 or $X,000 per project; weeklong at $XX,000 - $XX,000; and $XX,000 to $X00,000 to complete an entire project.

13. One Day _____ Club Sponsors, and sponsors of longer projects, do receive free t-shirts and a lunch.

14. Sponsors are invited to any type of celebration for their completed project (such as dedication, grand opening, or Open House) as an act of stewardship to build upon the relationship.

The main idea is to not only accept single volunteers from your website, phone calls, or walk-ins, but to strategically research different groups (corporations, faith, education, civic groups, neighborhood associations, etc.) to create groups made up of as many volunteers that are needed to complete the project. The more group project days that you can fill will significantly increase the number of volunteer hours.

In addition, call and request a visit with any of the individuals who sign up automatically on your organization's web page or Facebook page or other online volunteer registry. Establish a policy that everyone will need to attend an initial project volunteer meeting. Just call it a change in procedures to improve the relationship. Never get tied up on the phone to explain the Sponsorship program because it will fail. Face-to-Face meetings are king. You will have a harder time getting sponsorships from the those who have volunteered for many years, but at least try. The idea is to drive your volunteer activity from individuals to groups. Ask individuals who want to volunteer for a day if they could form a group from their work, civic organization, or church/temple/mosque. If they cannot, then let them volunteer for a day as usual; you don't want to lose them. The idea is to get more groups rather than "stray" individuals. This program will not work if there is no one willing or trained to complete face-to-face visits or meetings. In addition, the DD or DC must have the courage and ability to request funding. Not everyone can do this.

On average, only ten percent will accept the newly proposed volunteer sponsorship program by written letter or e-mail, 40 percent over the phone, and more than 80 percent in person. The processes should be followed as closely as possible. If you are the one making the requests and need more time, then you should try to have your most reliable staff members and/or volunteers cover your other administrative duties. You will now be spending more time with volunteers and development. Please note that the rules stated here are very important. People will come up with an endless number of exceptions to the policy and procedure guidelines. It seems once you begin to bend the rules, all chaos occurs.

9

INITIAL CONTACT, COMMUNICATION, & THE WAIT

This section is devoted to researching and establishing meetings with groups. Shifting from individuals to setting up meetings with organizations is a numbers game. At my second employer, I needed to call ten organizations to get four callbacks and two one-on-one visits. I wanted ten face-to-face meetings a month. The name and brand of my organization were not popular and people did not get cuddly feelings about the people we served. I found at my third employer that when I called ten organizations, I got six callbacks and four meetings. Their name and brand represented a quality mission, vision, and business model. So now, when I call, I do not feel one bit sheepish. We are a company that businesses want to invest in both financially and physically, and will at least listen to what I have to say. I now better understand the credibility of an organization or company's brand name and logo on the fundraiser/ development director's position.

Start by creating an Microsoft® Excel file to keep track of the name of the group, representative, phone, e-mail address and other contact information, and notes. Organization is crucial for keeping track of the many contacts you will establish and need to refer to for future fundraising campaigns. Review groups in your database, along with area Chambers of Commerce membership lists, etc. I research online for area companies with at least 40 employees, or those with branches which could lead to a group of 8-15 volunteers or whatever your group requirements may be. I will even look at the names of organizations on building signs and research them. I locate the manager's or director's name and set up a meeting. I try to never go in blind or complete a cold call. Often, I tell the operator what I am calling about and they will transfer my call to the right person. I try to go right to the top, but will talk to lower level management. I usually complete phone calls on Tuesday, Wednesday or Thursday. Mondays and Fridays are not good days to make calls. I may try calling from 10 a.m. to 11 a.m. If I cannot reach anyone during that time, then I stop right there and choose a different day and time. I sometimes hit a great combination of a day and time and get ahold of everyone in an hour's time and set several appointments. I do not leave messages because then my request is controlled by someone else, and will leave you waiting for a return call and wondering for days.

I call and tell them who I am and ask if I can set up an appointment with the best representative of their organization or company. They will ask why you want to meet with them. You answer that you have an opportunity for them to help people in need of their service. Again, do not get caught trying to explain the program over the phone instead of in person with your properly prepared materials.

If they state that they will call back, note that you called on your Excel file list and then wait. This waiting period causes the <u>first problem</u> as they are now in control, which is bad. They may direct you to someone else and that is good. You will at least meet and gain a foot in their door. It is great to have ten visits a month to prospects. You are both trying to increase volunteers and funding. I usually meet them at their workplace and rarely over lunch because there are too many distractions. The problem is that your list begins to grow of those whom you are meeting, those whom you are waiting on, and so forth. It can get confusing, so organization in your Excel file is very important. I eliminate the prospects that I think are dead ends so I can concentrate on the good ones. It is very unfortunate when they have to cancel the meeting and you begin all over again. You are heading down the right path by continuing to create lists of new groups, organizations, and company contacts and calling them to set up meetings. Getting out of the office and meeting community leaders is one of the most important tasks in fund and volunteer development.

ADDENDUM D. VOLUNTEER LOG

			Company XYZ Volunteer Log			
			Called-Yellow Tab			
			Date Set Non-Paid-Purple Tab			
			Date Set Paid-Green Tab			
			Cancelled by Group-Blue Tab			
			Cancelled by XYZ Company-Orange Tab			
			Red Listed-Non Reliable			
# Days	$	Paid	Volunteer Group Target List	Contact	E-Mail	Phone

10

ONE-ON-ONE REQUESTS

This is an explanation of how I complete requests from my 30 years of fundraising and development experience. First of all, it took about 15 years to switch my one-on-one meeting approach from a request or a sales pitch to a conversation. I changed from doing all the talking to asking questions and listening to the answers and building the conversation from there. My new coordinator was fascinated while being a part of a few one-on-one requests that I made. The coordinator said that I was so smooth and it did not feel uncomfortable at any point. I call prospective donors and make an appointment. I post the appointment on my calendar with the address, name of person to meet, and phone number just in case I am running late. I arrive ten minutes early, dressed appropriately; I wear a business suit for a meeting with a banker, or jeans and a company shirt to meet with a grain company representative. When I walk in I always ask for a bottle of water. It helps to take a drink if you get nervous and it shows that you are not afraid. It allows for the person you are meeting to grab a bottle or some coffee. As I walk in to the person's office, I look on the walls or desks for photos of pets, golfing, fishing, deer racks or anything indicative of interests and hobbies. It could be a family photo and you can talk about kids. I always start off the conversation far away from my reason for being there. You control the conversation carefully. Hopefully, you get someone who is light hearted and plays along. There is nothing worse than getting a serious and busy person who just wants to get down to business. Then you have to just complete the pitch and hope for the best. With the more easygoing person you might mention, "Wow that is a big fish," when you see his photo from a fishing trip. "Where did you get it?" Then you add a story about one of your fishing excursions. You ask where they like to vacation, where they fish, and just keep it personal and light. You want them to feel comfortable and connected to you. Then state that you are with the XYZ company and your position. Ask them if they ever volunteered or helped the XYZ company in any way. Then ask if their company or organization gets involved with volunteer projects. Ask if there any type of organization giving program. Describe your mission and business model. Tell him that you have an ***urgent*** need for more volunteers and funding to accomplish more projects quickly.

At some point during your visit, you are going to have to slowly walk through the request pages with the person you are meeting. They can be created on any type of graphic design software. Make sure the name of the project is creative and use photos of your projects. The first page should represent the project and the amenities of the project day or what they get. The second page should be the different levels of request for sponsorship funds. The third page you may not need because it states all the reasons why the volunteer software system is important. The fourth page is optional and concerns the use of a peer-to-peer fundraising tool. We found that some companies or individuals who make up a group have no way to sponsor, but they accept fundraising themselves via a peer-to-peer campaign system. It takes some time to get into it and learn and how to set up your campaign.

Walk through it page by page. Be bold enough to go through the giving levels. Ask them if they ever let their employees volunteer during working days. Gauge how they seem at this point. Ask them if they think their employees would get excited to volunteer for a one-day project. Try to ask three questions that you know they will answer with a yes. This keeps it positive. Ask, "Would you ever consider setting up a one day project and sponsor the event?" Then stay quiet until he responds. You are only asking them if they would consider it. If he/she is negative, then coast away from the request and back out slowly. Focus then on just completing a day of volunteering. If they say that it would be considered or they had to approach a committee or needed to get their boss's approval then thank them. Ask when they will get back to you with a decision. Ask if his/her company would be able to do both the volunteer day and the sponsorship gift. If they agrees to both, then walk through the giving levels and ask which level they feel they could support. It is best to get that amount, but most often the company has to approve it. Take your volunteer schedule and try to pinpoint a day or days they could work. It is best to get that day while you are there, but this most often does not happen. It is best to give a group at least a three-week lead time before the project. Then you incur your <u>second problem</u> of putting them onto your other wait game list of setting a date. Unfortunately, I often have five to ten organizations on this list. It is so hard to get a company to pull themselves away from what they do to commit to a project, even a volunteer fun day. I do find that it is best to post a full set of meeting notes into your donor database program. There is no way to remember everything said when you are involved with keeping track of multiple potential companies, companies you are waiting to hear back from, and the groups that already have a volunteer project date. You can refer to these notes before you communicate with them again. Practicing and getting proficient at requesting funding and volunteers in a one-on-one meeting is a very valuable step in this new program.

11

AFTER THE REQUEST

You will need to organize your group lists and points of contact in order to drive them to a volunteer date and sponsorship amount. You end up having a mess on your hands between waiting for the group to get back after a call, waiting to meet and the ones that you met with and are waiting on a date selection or sponsorship. I usually can wait one week to two months to get a message back that they selected a date. I have lost several companies after the empowerment of the meeting wears off.

Set up "canned" or pre-written follow-up e-mails that you use for each step:

1.) An initial thank you for meeting, a reminder of the dates and sponsorship amount they were looking at or inform them of all possible dates.
2.) A reminder that you would like to schedule their date and gift.
3.) Thank you for the date and information required for the project.

4.) An e-mail that the companies can send to their employees to get them to register for a volunteer project date.

Managing several different contacts along the entire communication process is a very important task.

12

THE IMPORTANCE OF THE TEAM CAPTAIN

It is very important that the company designate a team captain that you will communicate with from the first point of the sign-up process to the day of the project. A team captain can make or break the project. The team captain most likely will not be the leader that you initially spoke with about the project. I suggest that you meet directly with this person to establish a relationship with him/her. My staff created a nice information packet containing the printed rules, a list of frequently-asked questions with answers, and a flyer on white paper that they can reprint in any color, along with advertising and sponsorship materials. First, the team captain must identify which employees are willing and excited about volunteering, then register them with a paper or electronic waiver. This process can be a very frustrating waiting time for you. You can send the team captain a general e-mail about the project for him/her to forward to company employees, in order to publicize the event and attract volunteers.

Sample e-mail:

We are excited to announce that (company name) is in a new relationship with (XYZ not-for-profit organization). Together, we can help XYZ (improve/increase) its community services. It only takes one day of your time to make a difference for someone that will last a lifetime.

We are going to host a one-day (project) on (date) from (time). You will be paid for the day. Two breaks will be provided, along with snacks and water. Our company is sponsoring the project with a gift of $_____ for the day so the XYZ not-for-profit will provide lunch at noon and provide (gift associated with your organization with the club name on it; for example, water bottle, t-shirt, etc.) and explain its mission. We will be invited to the (dedication, grand opening, etc.).

Sample letter for prospective donors:

Date

Your organization/non-profit's name and return address

Dear xxx,

Is your organization, group, or business looking for a service project that you can tackle as a team? We can help!

Many people from all walks of life have volunteered as a team to help XYZ not-for-profit organization provide services to the community. You will work side-by-side with your community members to help make someone's dream a reality.

Volunteer close to home. The current project is listed on our website, www.xxxx. Click the sign up button to register (to your website paper waiver registrant spot). If you have questions just call (name) at (phone number).

Sincerely,
(your name and title)

13

PAPER OR ELECTRONIC WAIVERS

If your organization requires liability waivers, this can cause other issues. Sometimes you find great team captains who fill your targeted volunteer slots immediately. Sometimes you have to hound the team captain to get the volunteer time slots filled. Be very clear; if you require a minimum of volunteers, you must try to register that many or you will compromise the policies if you accept fewer. You can suggest options, like inviting employees' spouses, family members, or friends. Remember that the site supervisor has set up materials and equipment for a certain number of volunteers for that day, so be sure there will be enough for everyone if the number of volunteers increases.

If using a paper liability waiver system, the DC should e-mail a .pdf copy of the waiver to the team captain, and he/she will need to send it to the newly-registered volunteers. You should set a deadline for the waivers, as to when you will pick those up or they will deliver them. Send and collect youth waivers if any employees are bringing along older children to volunteer as well.

There are several inexpensive electronic web-based volunteer programs, which can make life easier for your organization. A web-based program can hold a lot of data and reports so that you will not need to spend so much time entering information. Just google "volunteer scheduling" and you can view the top ten companies and their systems. Prospective volunteers can visit your organization's website via their phone/computer/tablet, and select a day and time to volunteer, and register, all in one step. You can pre-set days for individual volunteers and save days that you are filling with the new sponsors. The sign-up process creates an electronic liability waiver. Working with a team captain can save a lot of time and confusion in the preparation and completion of the project.

14

SPECIAL AMENITIES

You need to develop levels of sponsorship gifts and accompanying items that donors will receive for each level of sponsorship. Be innovative and always have several different types of promotional items associated with your organization. For each increasing gift level, you need to add amenities. Be mindful in the cost of the items per sponsorship level; this will help both in developing a smart budget and increasing the value for each higher level.

In the sample below, the corporations, faith, educational, or civic groups that do sponsor get the following gifts per level.

Here is a sample of a listing that could be used on your printed donor request materials:

$X,000 Independence
Your contribution will fund our (program).
Participants each receive a box lunch, water, and _____Club t-shhirt.

$X,000 Strength

Your contribution will fund our (program).

Participants receive a box lunch, water, and _____Club t-shirt.

+Organization will also receive a written press release, along with Facebook and web posts.

+Participants will receive a bonus of a continental box breakfast

$X,000 Knowledge

Your contribution will fund our (program).

Participants receive a box lunch, water, and _____Club t-shirt.

Organization will also receive a written press release, along with Facebook and web posts.

Participants receive a bonus of a continental box breakfast.

+Organizations will also receive ten VIP tickets for the event's dedication or grand opening special event.

+ In addition, your organization will receive a Recognition Plaque for its efforts.

You can create other amenities to offer corporate sponsors. It is very important to follow through with each of these items. We have a stewardship plan where we send each donor sector something twice a year, like a letter of thanks with no request. We invite the groups to the dedication of the project they worked on, or create a special event (such as a cookout or party event) to which they are all invited. Employees like the chance to volunteer for a worthwhile cause because they feel like they are paying back what they received from the organization. Treat the sponsors well, then it will be easier to approach them the next year. You do not want to be in a position where you only see them the day that you make the annual request.

15

THE DAY OF THE EVENT

There are some tasks associated with a sponsored day of a volunteer project. Be prepared to take photos of the group in which you can send them after the project is over. Volunteers groups always like to have materials for their own promotional needs. You will need to take some time to round up the food, T-shirts, plaques and any other amenities before the day of the event. If it is food, then set up a good deal with a food provider for a breakfast, snacks, lunch or dinner. Make sure you ask if there are any dietary needs. Be sure to come early and that the site supervisors knows when to break for breakfast, lunch or evening dinner. Build a good relationship while visiting with them so they know you and will be especially careful to get the order right. I normally give a short mission speech so that that know more about the organization than they did before. They know you will be coming back. Call and make order the day before and pay then or if required when you pick it up.

16

DEDICATION/GRAND OPENING

I t is great to provide ample notice of the dedication of your project's completion for the groups that sponsored it. Most do not attend, but it is a nice gesture to make them feel recognized and appreciated. Make sure to get the approval of the client if appropriate. Provide a map attached to the e-mail to the team captain of the group. Tell a story about the client. They can forward that message to their team. Make sure to get RSVP's by using a link to an "Eventbrite" schedule system, or something similar that provides an easy way to keep track of those who plan to attend, or not attend.

17

STEWARDSHIP

Any good not-for-profit should have an ongoing separate stewardship program. It is a process by which you can inform, invite, thank, and involve every sector of donors throughout the year. There is never a request within a stewardship piece, but words of praise and information about your organization's programs. There is an expense for a good stewardship program software, but with creativity, you can establish one for very little funding. Research "stewardship" and you will find ample materials as to how to build a good process. If you thank every donor sector twice a year, then approaching them for a gift will not be so hard. You never want to be in a place where the only time you see or communicate with a donor is with a gift request. Here are the ways that an organization can steward their volunteer teams:

E-mail a thank you note with photos of the day.
Mail volunteers hand-colored thank you notes from the children of clients served.

Send a packet of seeds to be planted to support an environmentally-related mission.

Send a letter with all the organization's accomplishments listed for the year.

Share how their volunteer actions helped your mission.

18

INVOICING

Invoicing is really important, but it is easy. Included is a sample of an invoice made on Microsoft® Word. Many other invoicing programs are also available. It is best to verify the sponsorship level and amount first before invoicing any company. Most organizations will require an invoice document. I usually leave the levels unmarked. If the level is unchecked, they may choose to increase their gift amount. I mail the invoice two weeks before the project so you may get donations prior to the project to help pay for the materials for that day. Sometimes I have to call if it has been awhile since I mailed the invoice and they have not sent the check. I set up a code system in our donor database and accounting software system titled with the project name so I can pull them up on a report list and call them next year to schedule another volunteer event. You will also be able to formulate budgets for your next year due to the fact that about 85% of the organizations return.

ADDENDUM E: INVOICE

TO:
Company Name
Address
City, ST, Zip

ATTN:
INVOICE #
INVOICE DATE:

EVENT DATE:

The (The LMB Beach Association) (Beachcomber Club) Invoice

(The LMB Beach Association) brings organizational volunteers together to complete a day of restoration to one of the world's best beaches. The LMB Beach Club not only provides an opportunity for our community to join in and clean beaches, but also to donate a sponsorship gift to help purchase much-needed equipment and supplies. In the end, it is a teambuilding experience where everyone goes home feeling like they accomplished so much!

Please place an X by your sponsorship level.

_____ $X,000 Blue Skies Level:
Participants receive a box lunch, water, and (Beachcomber Club) flip-flops.

_____ $X,000 Coral Reef Level:
Participants receive a box lunch, water, and (Beachcomber Club) flip-flops.
Organization will also receive an electronic press release to distribute to area media about this special volunteer event, along with Facebook and web posts.
Participants will receive a bonus of a continental box breakfast.
+Organizations will also receive ten VIP tickets for the event's dedication or grand opening special event.
+ In addition, your organization will receive a recognition plaque for its efforts.

_____ $X,000 Sand Castle Level:
Participants receive a box lunch, water, and (Beachcomber Club) flip flops.
Organization will also receive an electronic press release about this special volunteer event to distribute to area media, along with Facebook and web posts.
Participants will receive a bonus of a continental box breakfast.
+Organizations will also get VIP tickets to the "Beach Fest" (date to be announced).
+ In addition, your organization will receive a Recognition Plaque for its efforts.

Thank you for your sponsorship gift! It would be great to receive the gift before the build date.
Sincerely,

Please mail your sponsorship gift in the enclosed envelope or to (name/address).

19

BUDGET

It does not take too much money when creating a new program to form clubs of volunteers. Basically it involves the cost of creating a logo of your new program and the base set of your program and request materials. Possibly the budget could include the printing of these materials if you do not have a nice color copier. Most of the budget will be associated with the ordering of the amenities/giveaways that the volunteers will receive. Try to keep all the promotion limited to your free web page, blogs, Facebook, and other electronic promotion. If your not-for-profit goes as far as to budget wages and benefits per development project, then take a time study for the first month and multiply by 12 months. Staff time will be the highest expense.

Here is a sample budget:

Revenue

20 - $1,000 sponsor groups

10 - $2,500 sponsor groups

8 - $5,000 sponsor groups

4 - $10,000 sponsor groups

<u>2 - $25, two-week long sponsorship groups, five days, ten volunteers, for total of 100 volunteers</u>

<u>44 groups of ten for a total of 440 sponsored volunteers</u>

$175,000 Total Revenue

Expenses

$750 to graphic designer/ad agency to develop of club logo and donation request materials

$1,250 for printing of materials

$2,000 for 200 lower level volunteer gifts @ $10 each

$1,500 for 100 increased level of volunteer gifts $@ $15 each

$1,600 for 80 increased level of volunteer gifts $ @ $20 each

$1,000 for 40 in upper level of volunteer gifts $ @ $25 each

<u>$3,000 for 100 for week long gifts @ $30 each</u>

$11,100 Total Expense without wages & benefits

$163,900 Net income without wages & benefits

$10,000 Wages & Benefits @ 20% of annual staff time, based on a $30,000 salary

$153,900 Net Income with wages & benefits

88% Net Income

Most of your expenses are variable, based on your sponsorship price per level and the number of groups you feel can sign up. Even your wages and benefits are variable and are always covered by revenue gained from your time expended in one-on-one meetings and by new sponsors.

Again, attempt to identify a vendor who will work with you on lowering the minimum number of promotional items along with giving you the best prices. Also speak with the vendor about shortening the order turnaround time so that you can place orders just in time for your project dates. This will help reduce your costs. Finally, by not dating t-shirts or any other giveaway items, you will be able to use all of them.

In my first year, I spent $3,000 on promotional giveaways and only had to spend $855 for more the second year because I was able to use the leftover (undated) t-shirts and other items.

The creation of a sponsorship volunteer program establishes a major organizational gift club which always provides a high net income percentage when compared to your usual 50% net income "special event," which most often utilizes more staff time.

20

CLOSING NOTES

I hope that I have given you a solid plan to enable you to make organizational changes to increase your volunteers and funding, while saving staff time. I find that the organization also will need to find new ways to round up new clients or areas to be served. In addition, more promotion of the new club will help other programs. Maybe the new funds will help to purchase of more tools, improved equipment and staff. I think, at least, you will have organized your volunteer schedule to accommodate more groups. Through you and your development staff, your organization should have met hundreds of new organizational representatives and built more relationships. Most likely, your organization should have strengthened your current volunteer base by getting out and meeting prospective volunteers and sponsors. As an after-effect of meetings, many other opportunities should develop. If your number of volunteers increase, then your mission incurs a major increase in service to your community. In addition, since you are actually creating a new request project, more funds are received. I wanted to provide a steps and a process, along with my experience, to increase the effectiveness of a new method to increase volunteers, and increase funding, while saving staff time. I hope that this book with this new volunteer process and sponsorhip can be used to help your organization improve its processes substantially.